D1571548

A GIFT FOR:

_____

FROM:

_____

This edition published in 2016 by Hallmark Gift Books,
a division of Hallmark Cards, Inc., Kansas City, MO 64141
under license from Adams Media.
Visit us on the Web at Hallmark.com.
All rights reserved.

Illustrations by Kathy Konkle.

Designer: Dan Horton

ISBN: 978-1-63059-898-3
BOK1051

Made in China
0917

LIFE HACKS

500+ Ways to Simplify Your Life

KEITH BRADFORD

Hallmark

Aadamsmedia

CONTENTS

INTRODUCTION

Congratulations! You've just opened the most helpful book on the face of the planet. Give yourself a big pat on the back, because your life is about to change for the better. You'll now be able to get free food on your birthday, catch a liar in the act, unclog drains, stop mosquito bites from itching, charge your phone faster, and even survive a zombie apocalypse!

Life hacks have been around since the dawn of time, but they've just never had a title attached to them—until now. I still remember the first life hack I ever used. When I was a kid, my grandma taught me an old trick that cured my hiccups within seconds. I was amazed! Well, I was mostly just happy to get back to playing soccer so quickly. But to this day, any time I get the hiccups, I still use her trick and, poof, they're gone.

I started to realize that my grandma wasn't the only person that had secret tricks like this up their sleeve. Everyone seemed to have their own kind of tip or shortcut they used to hack their way through life. But imagine you could take everyone's tips, tricks, and shortcuts and put them all in one place; how great would that be? Oh wait, that's right, that's the book you're holding right in front of you!

Each of these life hacks have been pulled from various sources around the Internet as well as from user submissions from my blog 1000LifeHacks.com. Along with these are a ton more of my favorites that I've saved specifically for this book. They're all broken down into categories, from technology to cures and solutions, so you can decide which aspect of your life you'd like to improve upon and start from there. It doesn't need to be read in chronological order, either; you can flip to any page and start hacking your life right now!

CHAPTER 1:

TECHNOLOGY

1 Running low on battery? Put your phone on airplane mode and it'll charge much faster.

2 Get the Wi-Fi password to almost anywhere by checking the comments section on Foursquare.

3 If you mess up recording a voicemail, press "#" to re-record it.

4 Accidentally close a tab in your Internet browser? Press "Ctrl + Shift + T" to reopen it.

5 Out of "AA" batteries? You can use a "AAA" battery and fill the gap on the positive side with a small ball of tinfoil.

6 iPhone pictures will be of better quality if you take the picture and then zoom in on the saved version rather than zooming in while taking the picture.

7 Keep your charger from bending or breaking, by sliding it into the spring from an old pen.

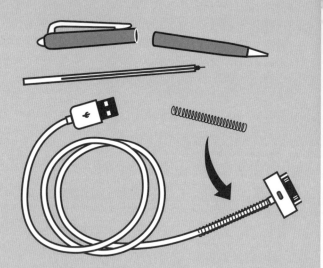

8 Storing batteries in the freezer can double their lifespan.

9 Dropped your phone in water? Put it in a bag of rice. The rice will absorb the water and can potentially save your phone from death.

10 If an image is burned into your plasma TV screen, turn on static for the entire day. The image will fade away.

11 If you have a computer that blocks sites like YouTube, Google Chrome's incognito mode will let you access them.

12 To resize a photo for Instagram, tilt your phone sideways and take a screenshot of it. It'll fit perfectly without affecting the quality.

13 Putting your phone on airplane mode will stop ads while playing games.

14 Swipe left or right on the iPhone calculator to delete the last digit so you don't have to start all over.

7 GOOGLE SEARCH HACKS

15 You can use Google search as a timer by typing in "set timer for" followed by the amount of minutes or hours you'd like Google to start counting down from.

16 Do you remember everything in your search term except for one word? Use an asterisk (*) in its place and Google search will fill in the blank for you.

17 Rather than sift through your local airport's website, simply type in the airline and flight number into Google search to get all the important information you need.

18 Turn the Google search page into pirate slang by typing in "Google pirate" and clicking the "I'm feeling lucky" button. "Settings" will now be referred to as "Me likes an' dislikes."

19 Want search results from one specific website? Type in your search term followed by "site:" and then the site you want the results from.

20 You can narrow your search to specific date ranges by typing in your search term and using ".." between the dates you want. For example, if you were searching for popular music during the mid-to-late 2000s, you could type in "Best albums 2004..2010."

21 Want to play Pac-Man? Go straight into the game by typing "Google Pac-Man" and clicking the "I'm feeling lucky" button.

22 When sharing headphones with friends, turn on the mono audio feature so that your phone splits the sound equally.

23 If you're in an area where you should have cell phone service but don't, put your phone on airplane mode and then switch back. This will cause your phone to register and find all the towers in your vicinity.

24 Your headphones can be used as microphones if you plug them into the mic jack on your computer. This is helpful when recording lectures.

25 Ever wonder why phone cords are so short? Using your phone while it's charging can damage the battery.

26 When letting someone use your iPhone to call someone, use Siri from the lock screen. They can call, but they can't look at your texts and photos.

27 Did your phone freeze? Plug it into a charger to free it up again.

28 Open an incognito tab in your browser and sign into Pandora to get unlimited skips for free.

29 Before you throw away a Post-it note, run it between the keys on your keyboard to collect dust, crumbs, and other things that might get trapped in there.

30 Make an autocorrect shortcut on your iPhone or iPad to easily enter your e-mail address.

31 If you play YouTube videos through Safari on your iPhone, you can still listen to them with your screen turned off.

32 Can't afford Microsoft Word? Get OpenOffice; it's the same thing except it's free and has a lot more features.

33 If your camera ever gets stolen, go to StolenCameraFinder.com. You can upload an old photo from your camera and it will show you if someone has been posting images with the same serial number on the Internet.

34 If you lost an Android phone in your house and it's on vibrate, you can find it by logging in to Android Device Manager online and clicking ring.

35 A quick and easy iPhone speaker using a toilet paper roll.

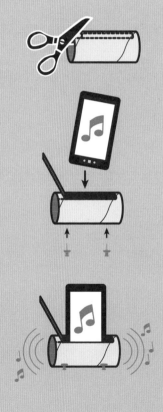

36 Drop a battery from six inches off the ground. If it bounces once and falls over it's still good. If it bounces around more than that, it's dead or on its way out.

37 When streaming Netflix on a computer, if the stream quality is sub-par, press "Control + Alt (Opt) + Shift + S" in order to change the buffering rates. Changing it to 3000 will give you HD video.

38 If YouTube is forcing you to sign in, delete everything after the last "v=" and then change "v=" to "v/".

39 Confused by a Wikipedia article? Click "Simple English" on the left list of languages and it'll whisk you to a simplified version.

40 Cleaning out your Windows computer? Search "size:gigantic" and it'll display all the files on your computer greater than 128mb.

41 Before going to a suspicious site, Google "safebrowsing:(website)" to see a ninety-day history of malware attempts on its visitors.

42 If your phone battery is really low and you need it for later, don't turn it off. Instead, put it on airplane mode. Turning it off and on will actually waste more battery than keeping it on airplane mode.

43 You can search "[month][year]" in Wikipedia to give you all the major world news for that month.

10 SITES YOU SHOULD BOOKMARK RIGHT NOW

44 On Supercook.com you can enter what ingredients you have readily available and it will tell you what meals you can make as well as how you can make them.

45 10MinuteMail.com gives you a fake e-mail address so you don't have to use your own personal e-mail address when signing up for things.

46 Have a song stuck in your head but can't think of the name? Midomi.com will find it based on what you sing or hum into your computer or phone.

47 On AccountKiller.com you can instantly remove all of your personal data from websites you don't want having it.

48 Want to learn how to speed-read? Spreeder.com is a free website designed to improve your reading speed and comprehension.

49 Don't have a ruler? iRuler.net gives you an actual-sized virtual ruler.

50 Want to know if the file you downloaded contains a virus? Upload the file to Jotti.org and they'll tell you if it's safe to open.

51 At PrintWhatYouLike.com you can make your own printer-friendly version of a website. Print only the essentials, and reformat the page to print exactly what you want.

52 CopyPasteCharacter.com allows you to copy and paste symbols and special characters like copyright symbols, arrows, foreign currency, accented letters, and many more.

53 You can send any size file online for free at PipeBytes.com without uploading to a third party server.

54 Put glow-in-the-dark paint on your phone charger so you'll never fumble in the dark for it again.

55 Turning the flash off on your cell phone camera can extend your battery life even when you're not actually using the camera!

56 Want to download a YouTube video as an mp3? Put "listento" after the "www." in the URL.

57 Use bread clips to label your power cords so that you can easily tell them apart.

58 Want to make sure you wake up in the morning? The Snooze app for iPhone will donate to charity each time you hit the snooze button.

59 Forgot your computer password? Boot up in safe mode (F8 during startup), log in as the administrator, and then change your password.

60 The Along the Way app will give you any cool attraction you can see along the way of any road trip.

61 When you copy something from the Internet use "Ctrl + Shift + V" to paste it. This will prevent the text from formatting.

62 In your e-mail inbox, search for "unsubscribe" to find all of the newsletters you never bothered to unsubscribe from.

63 Need to remember something in the morning? Send yourself a text before you go to bed, but don't open it until the next day.

64 You can use the volume + button on your iPhone ear buds to take a photo.

65 By charging your laptop battery only up to 80% instead of 100%, you can greatly extend the usable lifespan of the battery.

66 Can't read the text on a website? Press "Control +" to zoom in on a PC and "Command +" to zoom in on a Mac.

67 When writing an e-mail, make sure the last thing you do is put in the recipient's e-mail. This will help you avoid sending an unfinished e-mail.

68 Turn any cord into a coil cord by wrapping it tightly around a pen and blow-drying it for two to three minutes.

69 When moving or redecorating, take a picture of the back of your TV or tech equipment to easily remember how everything hooks up.

70 To skip a YouTube ad, just change "youtube" to "youtubeskip" in the URL of any video.

71 When signing up for a website, don't answer the security questions honestly. You'll actually protect your account and identity more if you always use the same wrong answers.

72 iOS 9 has a built-in horizontal and vertical leveler. Open the compass and swipe to the left to access it.

73 The FastCustomer app will never make you wait on hold again. It calls the company for you, waits on hold, and then calls you when an actual human is on the line.

74 The program DeTune will transfer all of the songs from an iPod or iPhone onto your computer.

75 Fix a scratched CD or DVD by rubbing a peeled banana on it and then buffing it out with the outside of the peel.

76 Try the Sleep Cycle app for the iPhone. This bio-alarm clock measures your sleep cycle and wakes you up at the lightest point in your sleep, meaning no more groggy mornings!

CHAPTER 2:
FOOD AND DRINK

77 Have leftover coffee from the morning? Use it to make coffee ice cubes, which will cool down your coffee without diluting it.

78 Run your bacon under cold water before cooking it. Doing so will reduce shrinkage by up to 50%.

79 If your water starts foaming over the pot when you're boiling it, pour in a couple tablespoons of olive oil. It'll stop overflowing almost instantly.

80 When making hard-boiled eggs, throw one teaspoon of baking soda into the water. The shell will come off without a problem once the egg is cooked.

81 Any citrus fruit like an orange, clementine, or grapefruit becomes easier to peel when you gently press and roll it on the table before peeling.

82 Poke a fork through the creamy part of an Oreo so that you can dip the whole Oreo in milk without getting your fingers wet.

83 Put pancake mix in an empty ketchup bottle for a clean, no-mess experience.

84 If you peel a banana from the bottom, you won't have to pick the little "stringy things" off of it.

85 Reheat leftover pizza on a frying pan. It'll keep the crust from getting soft.

86 When it comes to staying awake, apples are actually more powerful than caffeine.

87 You can ripen your avocados more quickly by placing them in a brown bag with bananas for 24 hours.

88 Trying to cut sugar out of your diet? Freeze bananas. They're much sweeter when frozen, making for a great, tasty treat.

10 FOODS THAT GET RID OF AN UPSET STOMACH

89 Bananas

90 Ginger

91 Plain yogurt

92 Papaya

93 Applesauce

94 Oatmeal

95 White rice

96 Chamomile tea

97 Chicken broth

98 Aloe vera juice

99 When you want to put a two-liter bottle of soda away, shake it up a little bit first. It will stay fizzy for weeks.

100 Ice cream too frozen to scoop? Don't microwave it; simply run the spoon under hot water.

101 Ketchup can be used to clean copper pots and pans. The acid in ketchup removes tarnish and makes copper shine.

102 Hate when your Hot Pockets explode in the microwave? Stab it with a fork before you put it in.

103 Wrap the stems of your bananas in plastic wrap to prevent them from browning so quickly.

104 Cottage cheese and sour cream will last twice as long if you turn the container upside down. This forms a vacuum seal and prevents bacteria from getting in.

105 To tell if an egg is fully cooked or raw, just spin it. If the egg wobbles, it's still raw. If it spins easily, it's fully cooked.

106 Microwaving lemons and other fruits for fifteen seconds can double the amount of juice you get from them.

107 You can use the lid of a yogurt or applesauce container when you don't have a spoon handy. You can also twist one of its ends to use as a handle.

108 Did your soda get shaken up? Tap the sides, not the top, to prevent bubble buildup and soda explosion.

109 Use frozen grapes to cool down wine without having to water it down.

110 Tired of jelly soaking through your peanut butter and jelly sandwiches? Spread the peanut butter on both sides of the bread and put the jelly in the middle.

111 Did your tortilla chips get a little stale? Toss them in the oven for 10 minutes at 375 degrees. They'll come out just like new!

112 An empty Pringles can makes for a perfect container for your raw spaghetti.

113 Put sprinkles in the bottom of the ice-cream cone to prevent leaks.

114 You can order Starbucks drinks at "kid's temperature." The drink will be much cooler and you'll never burn your tongue again!

115 Need to cook a whole bunch of hot dogs at once? Toss them all in a Crock-Pot.

116 To keep potatoes from budding, toss an apple in the bag.

117 Want to stop crying when chopping onions? Just chew gum.

118 Making cookies and don't have eggs? Sure, you could ask the neighbor, but half a banana (per egg) works as a great substitute.

119 Want to make a drink cold really fast? Wrap it in a wet paper towel and put it in the freezer for two minutes.

120 You can unroll the rim of ketchup cups to increase their capacity.

121 Buying ice cream? Press on the top of the container. If it's solid, it's been properly stored. If it can be pushed down, it's been thawed and refrozen.

122 Want to cut a watermelon open without a knife? Take a quarter, make a small incision at the center of the watermelon, and karate chop it in half. No joke, it actually works!

123 Make stale cookies soft again by putting them in a plastic bag with a piece of bread. Leave it overnight and they'll be almost good as new.

124 Push a straw through the middle of a strawberry to easily remove the stem.

125 Open your bag of chips from the bottom, since most of the flavoring has sunk there.

126 Before frying, sprinkle a little salt in your pan. This will help keep the oil from splattering.

127 When heating leftovers, space out a circle in the middle of the food. The empty space will help your food heat up much more evenly.

128 Stuff marshmallows before you roast them. The possibilities are endless, but chocolate chips, peanut butter cups, and strawberries are always great fillings.

129 To make BLTs, or any toasted sandwich, place two slices of bread in a single toaster slot. This way, the bread gets toasty on the outside, but stays soft and chewy on the inside.

130 How to avoid rotten eggs.

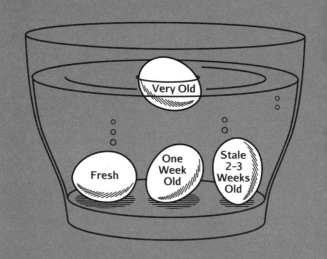

131 Tired of messy cake cutting? Run your knife under hot water, dry it off, and then cut your cake. Works like a charm. You may need to re-heat it a few times if you're cutting a whole cake.

132 Drinking a cold glass of water in the morning will wake you up faster than a cup of coffee.

133 Bake your cookies in a muffin tin. They'll stay soft and fluffy, and won't spread out as thin as they normally would.

134 You can add two eggs and half a cup of oil to turn any cake mix into cookie dough.

135 It's completely safe to eat the stickers that are on fruit. Even the glue used to put them on is food grade.

136 Has your champagne lost its bubbly-ness? Drop a raisin in and watch the bubbles magically return.

137 Use waxed, unflavored dental floss to cleanly slice a cake.

138 Take a sip of your coffee before adding in sugar. You won't need as much sugar for it to taste as sweet afterward.

139 Can't get that garlic smell off your hands? Rub them on stainless steel for 30 seconds before washing them.

140 Place a piece of wax paper on top of your ice cream to prevent freezer burn.

141 Before cutting up a pineapple, place it upside down in the freezer for thirty minutes. Since all the sugar sinks to the bottom of the fruit, this disperses it.

CHAPTER 3

HEALTH AND FITNESS

142 When you feel the urge to drink or smoke, go for a run, do twenty sit-ups, or some other activity that will get you moving. You'll soon start to associate quitting the habit with being fit.

143 Gatorade and Powerade are only healthy when used during a workout, and watered down. Otherwise, it's mostly extra sugar and empty calories.

144 When you're thirsty and limited water is available, rinse your mouth for thirty seconds before swallowing. Most of your "thirst" comes from a dry mouth.

145 Exhale when your left foot hits the ground to avoid cramps while running.

146 Drinking two cups of water before meals can make you lose an average of four and a half more pounds in twelve weeks.

147 Recipe for relaxation: Exhale completely, inhale for four seconds, hold your breath for seven seconds, and exhale for eight seconds.

148 Listening to music while working out can boost your running and lifting ability by 15%.

149 Eating a small amount of chocolate in the morning can actually help your body burn calories and lose weight throughout the day.

150 A cup of coffee before a workout speeds up the fat burning process.

151 Getting the right amount of sleep is crucial for your immune system. Sleeping for more than nine hours at a time can actually damage it!

152 Eliminate stress and headaches by resting in this position for five minutes.

5 SIMPLE WEIGHT-LOSS TIPS

153 Drink more water.

154 Adjust your portion sizes.

155 Lower your sugar intake.

156 Limit carbs to one time per day.

157 No fast food.

158 Skipping meals can cause your body to go into a fat-storing starvation mode, making it harder to burn calories.

159 Because of their high lycopene content, eating tomatoes may help prevent sunburns.

160 Drinking sixteen ounces of water will increase your metabolism by up to 30%.

161 Want to lose weight? Don't eat anything four hours before you go to bed. It makes a huge difference.

162 Cold showers may help relieve depression and will keep your skin and hair healthy.

163 Eating breakfast in the morning makes it ten times easier to burn calories throughout the day. It also makes you less likely to get acne.

164 The more organized you are, the less likely you are to develop Alzheimer's disease.

165 Eating celery is technically exercise. When you eat celery, you burn more calories digesting it than you consume.

166 Pineapple juice is five times more effective than cough syrup. It also prevents colds and the flu.

167 If you want good running form, try to run as quietly as possible. You'll be able to run faster and longer.

168 The cells in your body react to everything that your mind says. Negativity actually brings down your immune system.

169 Drinking five cups of green tea in a day can help you lose weight around your belly.

170 Yawning actually cools down your brain, which helps get rid of stress.

10 REASONS YOU SHOULD DRINK MORE WATER

171 It increases energy and relieves fatigue.

172 It helps your body lose weight.

173 It reduces your risk of getting kidney stones or a UTI (urinary tract infection).

174 It improves your skin's complexion.

175 It helps digest your food, preventing constipation.

176 It boosts your immune system.

177 It acts as a natural headache remedy.

178 It prevents cramps and sprains by keeping your joints lubricated.

179 It puts you in a good mood.

180 It saves you money! Water is free. In fact, fast food restaurants legally have to give you water for free if you ask.

181 Smiling for sixty seconds, even when you're in a bad mood, will immediately improve your mood. Using these muscles is enough to trigger the happy chemicals in your brain.

182 Always exercise on Monday. This sets the psychological pattern for the rest of the week.

183 Need some motivation to go to the gym? GymPact is an app that will pay you for working out and punishes you for missing out on days.

184 When you find yourself looking in the fridge out of boredom, drink the biggest glass of water you can find. You'll be too full to want food.

185 Drinking chocolate milk has been proven to help relieve muscle soreness after a workout.

186 Stretch for five minutes before going to bed. Your muscles will be more relaxed and it'll be easier to find a comfortable position to sleep in.

187 If you're going for a run, the jog.fm app will select a music playlist for you based on your pace.

188 Don't wet your toothbrush after you put toothpaste on it. Water reduces some of the healthy benefits of using toothpaste.

189 Eating plenty of unsalted sunflower seeds is a great home remedy for reducing your cholesterol level.

190 Want to lose weight? Eat more spicy food. Spicy foods trick your taste buds into being more satisfied with smaller amounts of food.

191 Drinking fruit juice doesn't even come close to the benefits of eating fruit. Fruit juice often contains more sugar and a lot less fiber.

192 Laughing for fifteen minutes has the same health benefits as getting two extra hours of sleep.

193 Trying to eat less? Use a smaller plate. It tricks your mind into thinking there's more food, and also limits what you can pile onto your plate.

194 Eat an orange before working out. Not only does it keep you hydrated, but it also prevents your muscles from getting sore.

195 When you're stressed, try eating 1 cup of low-fat yogurt or 2 tablespoons of mixed nuts. The amino acids in them will help calm you down.

196 Daytime naps help to improve your memory and cut the risk of heart disease.

197 By thinking one positive thought every morning, you can psychologically train yourself to be a happier person.

198 Learning to play a musical instrument or learning another language can actually slow down the aging process of the human brain.

199 Working out before bed makes your muscles burn more calories throughout your sleep cycle.

200 You can use a tube sock as a simple workout armband.

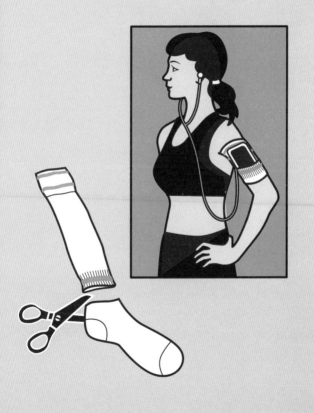

201 When you're feeling down or depressed, do some cleaning. Straightening out the physical aspects of your life can also bring clarity to the mental ones.

202 If you're stressed, try running. Outside of meditation, it's one of the best ways to clear your mind.

203 Mustard and toothpaste will help ease the pain of minor burns.

204 Doing 7,000 jumping jacks burns enough calories to lose about one pound. Spread that over a week and you'll lose an extra pound every week.

205 In order to lose a pound of fat, you'll have to run for more than 3 hours. If you run for 27 minutes every day, you can lose a pound in a week.

206 Got stung by a bee? Apply a cut onion to the area. This will help break down the chemicals responsible for inflammation and discomfort.

207 Make your playlists as long as you plan to exercise. This will make you focus more on your workout and keep you from constantly looking at the clock.

208 Don't want to miss leg day? Use the rowing machine. It works legs, arms, and abs.

CHAPTER 4
CURES AND SOLUTIONS

209 Mosquito bite? Apply a hot spoon onto the spot. The heat will destroy the reaction and the itching will stop almost instantly.

210 Candles will burn longer and drip less if they are placed in the freezer for a few hours before using.

211 Have a splinter? Pour a small amount of white glue on the area. Let it dry and peel it off. The splinter should come right out.

212 Don't want to be embarrassed when buying something? Buy an inexpensive birthday card with it.

213 Got a headache that just won't go away? Take a lime, cut it in half, and rub it on your forehead. The throbbing should go away.

214 If you want to get rid of bad breath, brushing your teeth is important, but what's more important is brushing your tongue.

215 Wrinkly shirt? Throw it in the dryer with a few ice cubes for five minutes.

216 You can heal paper cuts and immediately stop the pain by rubbing ChapStick on the wounded area.

217 Getting nauseous from reading in the car? Tilt your head side to side and it'll go away.

218 If you have sensitive ears, put Vaseline on earrings before putting them on. This should prevent irritation.

219 Use a clothespin while hammering. You'll never bang your thumb again!

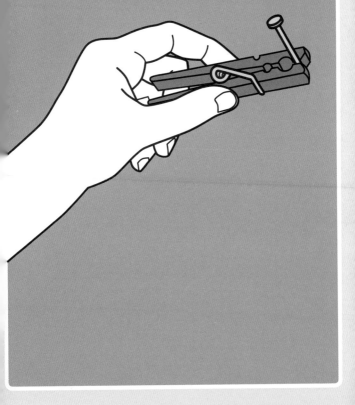

220 To stop a Popsicle from dripping on your hands, pierce a muffin cup liner with the stick so it catches the drizzle before it hits your hands.

221 Drinking a tablespoon of apple cider vinegar will relieve allergy and asthma symptoms.

222 Standard blackboard chalk will remove grease stains. Simply rub the stain with the chalk and toss it in the wash like normal.

223 Not sure if you have bad breath? Lick your wrist and smell it. This is what your breath smells like to others.

224 Runny or stuffy nose? Push your tongue against the top of your mouth and push a finger between your eyebrows. Hold it for about twenty seconds. Your nose should clear.

225 Gum stuck to your clothes? Boil vinegar and pour it over the gum. Use a brush to wipe off. The gum will come off instantly!

226 If you have painful gas, lie on your back and lift your knees to your chest. You'll fart it right out.

227 You can use toothpaste to easily remove crayon marks from walls.

228 To cure a sore throat, add a teaspoon of honey to JELL-O mix and heat it up. The gelatin will coat and soothe your throat.

229 Need some change? Put your cash into a vending machine and hit the coin return button without ordering anything.

230 Want to use your phone in the rain or on the beach? Put it in a Ziploc bag. The touch screen still works under the plastic and you'll still be able to hear the person on the other line.

231 Turn your steering wheel 180 degrees before parking in the sun. This way, you won't burn your hands when you start driving.

232 If you ever want to stop a sneeze from coming, simply press your tongue against the roof of your mouth and it'll vanish.

233 Accidentally get deodorant on your shirt? Rub a dryer sheet over the area to remove it completely.

234 Soak a cotton ball in vinegar and put it on a bruise to make it disappear.

235 Instead of scraping ice off your car, try spraying it with a mixture of ⅔ cup vinegar and ⅓ cup water. The ice will melt right off.

236 Flattened pillow? Put it in the sun for thirty minutes. The sun will absorb any moisture caught in the pillow and plump it up.

237 Are your thoughts keeping you awake at night? Try writing them all down. This clears your head and makes it easier to fall asleep.

238 Rubbing alcohol will remove pen marks and stains from pretty much anything.

239 The best way to cure hiccups is to actually try to hiccup.

240 Shoes too small? Put on three pairs of socks, put the shoes on, and blow dry for ten minutes. They'll fit perfectly now!

241 Put toothpaste on a pimple and it will disappear overnight. Make sure to use white toothpaste, though.

242 Wrap rubber bands around the ends of coat hangers to prevent dresses from slipping off.

243 Accidentally text the wrong person? Immediately put your phone on airplane mode and once it fails to deliver, delete the message.

244 Placing an envelope in the fridge for an hour will unseal it. Good tip to know if you forget to include something in a package.

245 Have a headache? Eating ten to twelve almonds is the equivalent of taking two aspirins for a migraine headache.

246 If you ever clog the toilet in a public restroom and there's no plunger, pour some liquid hand soap in. Let it sit for 5 minutes and flush again. This could save you someday.

247 To remove gum from your hair, dip the strands into a small bowl of Coke for a few minutes. You should be able to wipe the gum off with a comb.

248 If a shirt or sweater has static cling, put a safety pin in it. The static will instantly go away.

249 Make homemade ice packs by adding one part rubbing alcohol to three parts water in a Ziploc bag. It will get cold but not hard, so you can easily wrap it around sore body parts.

250 If you stand up too fast and start to black out, tighten your abs as hard as you can.

251 Hate getting those squeaky, wobbly, or bumpy carts at the grocery store? Try grabbing one from the parking lot before you enter the store. People usually ditch the bad ones inside, and it also gives you a chance to test it out before you start shopping.

252 It may sound crazy, but white wine will actually take out a red wine stain.

253 Drinking two glasses of Gatorade can relieve headache pain almost immediately, without the unpleasant side effects caused by traditional pain relievers.

254 Put clear nail polish onto the outer threads of a button to keep it from unraveling or popping off your jacket or sweater.

255 Have an itchy mosquito bite? Put some Wite-Out on it. The correction fluid will stop the itch within seconds!

256 When a bag of chips is stuck in a vending machine, don't buy the same bag again to unjam it; buy something right above it.

257 When you are at the pool or beach, set your flip-flops face-down. This prevents them from being scalding hot from the sun when you're ready to leave.

258 Pimple too painful to pop? Put it under hot water for a few seconds. This softens it and makes it easier to pop.

259 If you're feeling nervous, start chewing gum. Your brain will reason that you're not in danger because you wouldn't be eating if you were.

260 Put a stocking over a vacuum cleaner attachment to find tiny lost items like earrings.

261 Remove gross, unpleasant odors in smelly shoes or gym bags by placing dry tea bags in them and leaving them there overnight.

262 Spam texts bothering you? Forward them to 7726 and your carrier will reply asking for the number it came from to help stop spam.

263 Ate something really spicy? Eating a teaspoon of sugar will completely neutralize the heat sensation.

264 If you wet your fingertips and the head of the nail clippers, the nail clippings won't fly off when you trim your nails.

265 Putting apple cider vinegar on moles, warts, and skin tags will remove them.

266 The gel from an Advil liquid gel will cure a pimple almost instantly.

267 If you accidentally over-salt a dish while cooking, drop a peeled potato into the mix. The potato will absorb the excess salt.

268 To instantly untangle headphones, pick a point about halfway along the wire and shake it.

269 Squeezing a lemon or lime into your shampoo will stop frizzy hair.

270 Acne Scar Remedy: Mix a teaspoon of nutmeg and a tablespoon of honey into a paste. Apply for thirty minutes and rinse. Repeat daily, if needed.

271 Want to cool down your body temperature? Run your wrist under cold water for at least five minutes. It'll cool your blood down.

272 Tired of getting between zero and seven Tic Tacs when you shake the container? Avoid that by letting the mint gently glide into the tiny crevice in the lid.

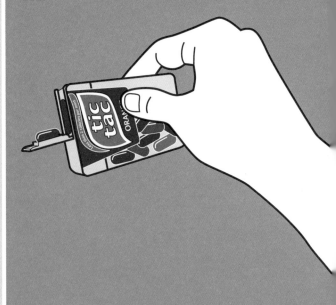

273 Having trouble sleeping? Look at photos of other people sleeping. This triggers a response in your brain that actually makes you feel more tired.

274 Stuffy nose? Leave a sliced onion near where you sleep and let it sit for the night. Your nose will be clear by the time you wake up.

275 Bad sunburn? Aloe lotion is good, but aloe ice cubes are better!

276 Immediately applying Mineral Ice Pain Relieving Gel to a burn will prevent blistering.

277 Take note of your body's position in the morning. This is probably your most comfortable sleeping posture, so posing this way before bed can help you get to sleep more quickly.

278 Get rid of fruit flies by filling a bowl with apple cider vinegar and a bit of soap. The vinegar will attract them and the soap will kill them.

279 If you're experiencing insomnia, drink a glass of raw lemon juice or a spoonful of honey before sleeping. This will drastically improve your sleep.

280 Remove a splinter by applying a paste of baking soda and water for several minutes. The splinter should pop out of the skin.

281 If you're out of shaving cream, use olive oil. It works just as well, if not better.

282 Have a sore throat? Try eating a piece of cucumber. It cools down your throat and stops that itchy feeling.

283 Need to get rid of the hiccups? Hold your breath and swallow three times.

284 Put a sticker with a fake PIN number on your debit card. That way, if you lose it and someone tries to use it more than three times, the machine will eat the card.

285 Get rid of rust by rubbing it with aluminum foil soaked in vinegar.

286 Zipper won't stay up? Flip it to the down position. This "locks" the zipper.

287 Can't brush after a meal? Gargle salt water. You'll be amazed at all the gunk that comes out!

288 Singing releases a large amount of endorphins in your brain and can make you feel better almost instantly.

289 Shoes smell funky? Use dryer sheets as an incredibly effective shoe deodorizer.

290 Cornstarch will untangle all kinds of knots. Rub some into shoelaces, chains, and string to easily loosen them up.

291 According to a study, smelling rubbing alcohol can relieve nausea almost instantly.

292 Need to get those annoying stickers off a product? Spray it with a liquid that contains alcohol, like perfume. Or just use rubbing alcohol. The alcohol eats at the glue adhesive, allowing for easy removal.

293 Hate insects? Take vitamin B complex during the summer to ward off mosquitos and biting flies.

294 Ate something too spicy? Drink milk. It will neutralize the spicy taste in your mouth.

295 Use toothpaste to clear up hazy car headlights—always works like a charm!

296 If you drop an earring, ring, or small screw, simply turn off the lights and look for it with a flashlight. It should light right up once you scan over it.

297 If you're a smoker and can't or don't want to quit, drink more black tea. It helps prevent the lung damage caused by smoking.

298 Did you know that it's beneficial to lick small cuts? A variety of compounds in human saliva can speed up healing.

299 The 20-20-20 Rule: Looking at something 20 feet away for 20 seconds every 20 minutes is a method proven to stop eye strain and headaches.

300 Suffering from acne? The problem could be your pillowcase. Sleeping on a fresh one every night will usually solve the problem.

301 Have a stomachache? Lie on your left side and rub your stomach in clockwise circles. It actually helps!

302 No bug repellent? Put dryer sheets in your shoes and in your pockets. It will help keep mosquitoes away.

303 Don't burn yourself with those hard-to-reach candles. Use a stick of raw spaghetti to light the wick.

304 Reading a book before bed makes your eyes tired. As a result, your brain is tricked into feeling tired and falling asleep is much easier.

305 The most effective cough syrup that exists is honey.

306 Have a headache? Submerge your feet and hands in hot water and put a bag of frozen peas on the back of your head. The heat on your extremities pulls the blood from your head, relieving your head pains.

307 Drinking a tablespoon of apple cider vinegar in the morning can help fight arthritis pain throughout the day.

308 Clogged drain? Unclog it with 1 cup of baking soda mixed with 1 cup of white vinegar.

309 Showering with cooler water can help stop dandruff.

310 Gum on your shoe? Spray it with some WD-40 and it'll come right off.

311 Blow some air in when filling up water balloons. This will cause it to pop when it hits someone instead of just bouncing off.

312 Do you have blue hands from your new jeans? Wash them with a tablespoon of salt to set the dye.

313 Get rid of your motion sickness by sucking on a lemon or eating olives.

314 Have a pounding migraine headache? Try eating spinach instead of popping a pill. Magnesium is used in the ER to treat migraine attacks, and spinach contains loads of magnesium as well as riboflavin.

315 Sleepy but don't want to be? Hold your breath as long as you can and then breathe out slowly. This will perk you right up!

316 When you feel like you're about to yawn, touch the roof of your mouth with your tongue to prevent it.

CHAPTER 5

MONEY SAVERS

317 If you bought something on Amazon and the price goes down within thirty days, you can e-mail them and they will send you the difference.

318 When grocery shopping, the cheapest items will be on the top and bottom shelves, not at eye level.

319 On the bottom of every Krispy Kreme receipt is a plea to fill out a survey. You get a free doughnut for doing the survey. When you get your doughnut, you get another receipt, with another survey. Free doughnuts for life!

320 You can get $100 off any vacation package from Delta Airlines if you book that trip during your birthday month.

321 LOZO.com will give you coupons for each item on your shopping list.

322 For frequent Starbucks customers: Buy and use a membership card. It only takes five transactions to get to the green level, and then coffee and tea refills are free.

323 Target will price match Amazon. If you find something cheap on Amazon, buy it at Target instead and you won't have to wait for it to be shipped to you.

324 Always ask for a discount when buying jewelry. You'll usually be able to get a good one.

325 In automatic car washes, the basic wash is just as good as the deluxe one. Those three-color soaps in the deluxe are just gimmicks, a ploy designed to get you to pay more for the same thing. All the actual cleaning of the car is done with regular soaps, which are included in every package.

326 You can get a free cup of Dippin' Dots during your birthday month. Just sign up for their e-mail and they'll send you a coupon!

327 Buying a gym membership? Most times your health insurance company will reimburse the cost for you, or at least provide a discount.

328 When shopping online, search for promo codes on Google before making a purchase. You can usually find a variety of discounts from free shipping to 25% off.

329 Never buy shoes again! Payless will replace any shoes you buy from them regardless of how long you've had them or what you've put them through.

330 Never go to the grocery store hungry. You'll end up buying several things you don't actually need.

331 If you have a gift card with less than $10 on it, the business is legally required to give you the rest of your balance in cash if you ask.

332 Buying a car? Buy it at the end of the month. Salespeople usually have quotas to meet and will be more likely to cut you a deal.

333 Download the Apple free app of the week, even if you don't need it. You can delete it and re-download it whenever you want for free!

334 When a price at Costco ends in $.97, it's their clearance price and that's the lowest it will ever go.

335 With the promo code "9ANY" you can get any pizza you want at Pizza Hut for $9 when you order online.

336 Put a binder clip at the end of your toothpaste tube to get every last bit.

337 Too broke to travel? WWOOF is an organization that allows you to travel the world, with food and accommodations covered, in exchange for volunteer work.

338 Most car washes have a rain check policy where if it rains within 48 hours of your last visit, you can get your car washed again for free.

339 Don't buy new ink cartridges for your printer. Take the old ones to Costco and get them filled for only $10.

340 On Halloween, any kid can get a free scary face Halloween pancake at IHOP.

341 If a Duracell battery leaks and destroys one of your devices, the company will replace the device if it's sent to them with the defective batteries still in place.

342 Don't pay to learn a new language! You can learn Spanish, French, Italian, German, and Portuguese for free on Duolingo.com.

343 If you cancel your Hulu Plus trial before the seven days are up, they'll give you the next month for free.

344 When going over 40 mph, it is more economical to have the windows up and AC on. While driving under 40 mph, the opposite is true.

345 While flying, sign up for the free thirty-minute trial of on-board Wi-Fi. Delete the cookies when trial ends and start a new trial.

346 If you have an ".edu" e-mail address, you can get a free Amazon Prime account. This lets you watch many TV shows and movies via Amazon.

347 Each 5 mph you drive over 60 mph is like paying an additional 10 cents a gallon for gas.

348 On Viberly.com, you can get a free subscription to Netflix or Spotify simply by putting a sticker on your laptop!

349 If you want to get a new laptop, phone, or other electronic device, get it in October. You can usually get up to 40% off most electronics.

350 On SNESFUN.com, you can play almost every single Nintendo game for free.

351 When buying something from Craigslist, use a fake e-mail address to lowball the seller by a lot. Then, using your regular e-mail address, offer a reasonable but still lower price. People will usually go for the second offer.

352 Starbucks offers an even smaller size than tall called a short. It's cheaper and a much healthier size.

353 At Chipotle, there's no limit to the number of tortillas you can order on the side.

10 PLACES TO GET FREE STUFF ON YOUR BIRTHDAY

354 IHOP: Free stack of pancakes.

355 Medieval Times: Free admission to the show when you sign up for the King's Court Club.

356 Dunkin' Donuts: Free cup of coffee.

357 Sephora: Free mystery makeup gift bag.

358 Cinemark Theatres: Free tub of popcorn.

359 Baskin-Robbins: Free scoop of ice cream.

360 Missouri: One free lottery ticket.

361 Waffle House: They offer a variety of free birthday meals.

362 Starbucks: Free drink if you're a rewards member (which is also free to sign up for).

363 Kmart: Free $5 to spend in their store.

364 Get your first Redbox movie rental for free! Just type in "dvdonme" when it asks for a promo code.

365 FuelMyRoute.com will tell you the lowest possible gas prices along your route.

366 When taking a cab somewhere unfamiliar to you, put your destination in your phone's GPS. This way, it will be impossible for the driver to scam you.

367 You can extend the length of a free trial by pushing back the date on your computer.

368 Several studies have shown that gasoline expands and contracts by 1% for every 15 degrees the temperature changes. It tends to be cooler in the morning, which means the gas is more contracted and you're getting more volume per dollar than when it's warmer in the afternoon.

369 If the taxi driver asks if you're "from around here," lie and say yes. Sometimes they drive farther (driving up the price) for tourists.

370 Grocery stores stack their products by sell-by date, which means the oldest food is in the front. Make sure to always grab food from the back.

7 THINGS
YOU SHOULD KNOW
BEFORE BOOKING
A FLIGHT

371 Use your browser's incognito tab or delete your history every time you go online to check flight rates. The prices actually go up when you visit a site multiple times.

372 Six to eight weeks before you want to book your flight is the cheapest time to buy.

373 The cheapest days to buy tickets on are Tuesday and Wednesday.

374 The cheapest days to fly on are Tuesday, Wednesday, and Saturday.

375 Sunday is usually the most expensive day to fly.

376 Prices change up to three times per day.

377 Discount ticket sales are usually offered at the beginning of the week.

378 The first Friday of June is National Doughnut Day. You can get a free donut at Krispy Kreme, no purchase necessary!

379 You can buy gift cards at up to 35% off their value from CardCash.com.

380 The Cinemark app will give you free popcorn vouchers and other rewards if you can keep your phone silent and screen dimmed during the movie.

381 If you send Mickey and Minnie Mouse an invitation to your wedding, they'll send you back an autographed photo and a "just married" button. Here is the address:

Mickey & Minnie
The Walt Disney Company
500 South Buena Vista Street
Burbank, CA 91521
USA

CHAPTER 6

LIFE TIPS

382 Fold your receipt around the gift card after you use it so that you always know your balance.

383 If you ever go to a zoo, wear the same colors as the employees do. The animals will come right up to you.

384 Put your home number in your cell phone's contact list under "Owner." That way, if someone finds it, they can easily contact you.

385 Take pictures of friends holding items you've lent them with your phone, so you remember down the road who borrowed what.

386 If your car is about to get towed, get in it. Tow trucks are forced to stop to avoid kidnapping charges.

387 When doing your nails, use Elmer's glue around your nail, let it dry, and then go crazy with the nail polish. Peel off the glue to reveal perfectly manicured nails.

388 Got invited to a wedding? Set the date as a recurring event in your calendar, so you can wish them a happy anniversary every year.

389 If you ever need to stop and ask for directions, skip the gas station and find a pizza delivery place. They know their way around town way better.

390 If you are buying headphones or speakers, test them out with "Bohemian Rhapsody." It has the complete set of highs and lows in instruments and vocals.

391 Listening to music literally changes your brain's perception of time and reduces the amount of time you think you're waiting. This is why they always have music playing in waiting rooms.

392 Never keep condoms in your wallet. After just a month in there, it has a 50% greater chance of breaking.

393 When flying with a group of friends or family members, make sure to mix up your clothing between the suitcases. That way, if a bag gets lost or stolen, one person isn't completely screwed.

394 For the best sound in a movie theater, sit two-thirds of the way back and as close to the middle as possible. This is where audio engineers sit when they mix sound for movies.

395 Microwave two big bowls at the same time by elevating the second bowl with a mug or another small, microwave-safe container.

396 Take a picture of yourself when your hair looks good. Show it to the barber the next time you get a haircut to ensure you get perfect hair every time!

397 Try and eat at least five home-cooked meals a week. A recent study shows that doing so makes you 47% more likely to live an extra decade.

398 Keep a card with all your emergency contact numbers and medical information on it in your wallet. It could save your life someday.

399 When you get a call from a telemarketer, don't say anything and press "9" on your phone. This will automatically add your number to their "don't call" list.

400 When buying something online, only read the reviews that gave three stars. They're usually the most honest about the pros and cons.

401 Put things back where you first looked for them, not where you found them.

402 You can call 311 for non-emergency calls to the police.

403 Try applying your deodorant at night instead of in the morning. It'll be more effective and you'll sweat less the next day.

404 If you ever have to park in a city at night, park in front of a bank. They're lit up and have cameras everywhere.

405 Don't know what to get someone for their birthday? Have them make three guesses of what you got them. You now have three ideas on what to get them!

406 When you're at a restaurant, wash your hands after ordering. The menu is generally the dirtiest thing you can touch.

407 Going to the beach? Clear out an old lotion bottle and put your phone, money, and keys in it for safer keeping at the beach.

408 Whenever you make a packing list for a trip, make two copies. Use one to pack and the second to make sure you bring everything back.

409 If you're walking in a bad area at night, call someone and stay on the line. If something happens, they can call the police.

410 Take a picture of business cards people hand you, just in case you lose them.

411 Never make the wrong turn on the freeway again: The alignment of the tabs on top of exit signs tells you whether the exit will be on the left or right.

412 Want to make sure you always get fresh fries at McDonald's? Ask for them unsalted. They'll make a fresh batch, and they also offer salt packages at the condiment counter.

413 Tie a small piece of brightly colored fabric to your luggage. You'll be able to spot your bag at the airport in no time!

414 If you're driving into a town and don't know what to do, call a hotel and say that you're staying there next week. They'll be more than happy to answer any questions that you ask.

415 If you're with Verizon, AT&T, T-Mobile, or Sprint, you can now text the police (911) in case of emergency.

416 If you ever find a driver's license, you can put it in any mailbox as is and the postal service will return it to its owner.

417 In a public bathroom, the stall that is the closest to the door is usually the cleanest because it's the least used.

CHAPTER 7

SURVIVAL

418 If you ever get kidnapped and they tie your hands together and put tape over your mouth, lick the tape. It will eventually fall off and you'll be able to yell for help.

419 If you're about to get hit by a car and can't jump sideways, jump up! It'll give you a better chance of surviving.

420 When you call 911, the first thing you should always say is your location. They immediately send police when they have an address.

421 Short on firewood? Make a Swedish Flame out of your remaining log. Make your cuts like you're slicing a cake. Leave about six inches at the base. Throw about half a cap of fuel oil in. It will burn for two to three hours.

422 Any working cell phone, regardless of whether it is in service or not, will call 911.

5 TIPS
FOR YOUR NEXT
CAMPING TRIP

423 Keep your toilet paper dry by putting it in an old CD spindle. It fits perfectly.

424 Use "joke candles" (the ones that can't get blown out) to light fires. This way, the wind won't affect the flame.

425 Blow into an acorn cap with your two thumbs over it if you ever get lost in the woods. This will make a loud high pitch whistling sound for other hikers or campers to hear.

426 Putting deodorant on an insect bite will stop the itch instantly.

427 Never get your matches wet. Store them in a small Tupperware container and glue a piece of sandpaper to the inside of the lid for a place to spark your matches on.

428 If you're on a road trip and can't pay for a motel, park at Walmart and sleep in your car. They won't kick you out!

429 Want to take a nap on public transit but are scared of getting your bag stolen? Put your leg through the loop or handle. If someone does try to take it, you'll feel them tugging at it.

430 If you ever suspect that someone is following your car, take four right turns. It will form a circle, and if they're still behind at that point, then they're definitely following you.

431 If you ever get stuffed in a trunk, disconnect the backlight wires. When a cop pulls them over or you're at a red light, kick the door so that people know you're there.

432 When using a riding mower on a slope, mow up and down, not sideways. About ninety-five Americans are killed each year because of not knowing this.

433 Need to give CPR? Compress their chest hard to the beat of "Stayin' Alive" by the Bee Gees. The tempo is the correct timing of compressions.

434 When you see a halo around the sun or moon, get indoors immediately. This means a storm is coming.

435 If you're in for a long drive at night, listen to comedians. It's impossible to fall asleep while laughing.

436 Don't put your feet up on a car's dashboard. Airbags go off like small bombs and can easily break both of your legs.

437 If you're outside in the woods and cut yourself, spider webs will not only seal the wound, but also make it heal much faster.

438 Doritos work great for kindling if you can't find any.

439 Find yourself without a source of fresh water? Get a cup full of dirty water and run a piece of cloth between that and an empty cup. After a few minutes, you'll have filtered, muck-free water. Remember to boil it before drinking.

440 Start a cooking fire easily by filling an egg carton with charcoal and lighting each corner.

441 Bees can't see you if you aren't moving.

442 Outside during a lightning storm? Avoid open fields, elevated mountaintops, and watery areas. Try to isolate yourself between rocks or in caves and never lie flat on the ground.

443 Whenever you're going on a camping trip, always make sure that someone who's not on the trip knows where you're going and when you'll be back.

444 Homemade Wasp Catcher: Cut off the top of a soda bottle, flip it over, and place it back onto rest of the bottle except upside down. Pour some sugar water into it and hang it in the area where you've had wasp problems.

445 Walking in a scary area at night? Download a police scanner app for your phone and listen to it on full volume.

CHAPTER 8

PARTY HACKS

446 How to open a beer with another beer.

447 Going to a bar? Start by giving the bartender a $20 tip. You'll get amazing service for the rest of the night.

448 Need a ride home on New Year's Eve? Call AAA insurance. They will pick anyone up and drive them home free of charge.

449 Always hold your drink in your left hand at parties. That way, your right hand won't be cold or wet when you shake someone's hand.

450 If you suspect someone's checking you out, yawn. If they yawn back, they were. Yawning is visually contagious.

451 Sprinkle salt on a napkin before putting a drink on it to prevent it from sticking to your cup.

7 TIPS FOR HOSTING A SUMMER BBQ

452 Save stovetop space: Cook corn on the cob in a cooler by pouring boiling water over the corn. Simmer for 5 minutes and serve. Don't leave them in for longer than 15 minutes or they will start to get tough.

453 Write your guests' meat doneness preferences on their buns with ketchup or mustard.

454 Serving punch? Make an ice block to keep it cool. It melts much more slowly than ice cubes.

455 Tie a bottle opener to the handle of the drink tub or cooler.

456 Always have bug spray and sunscreen handy.

457 Use a muffin tin for a cute and original condiment tray. Plus, it makes for an easy cleanup.

458 Adding two handfuls of salt to a cooler of ice water will chill drinks much faster.

459 Flip a pizza box around on your lap so when opened the lid covers your chest. You now have made yourself a Pizza Bib!

460 Look at someone's elbow when you high-five. You'll never miss again.

461 If you ever have to clean up vomit (and hopefully you don't), put ground coffee on it first. It takes away the smell and dehydrates it. Then, you can just sweep it up.

462 Tape pool noodles to the edge of a container. Add some ice and your favorite drinks for a homemade floating cooler.

463 You can clear a room full of cigarette smoke in about a minute by spinning a wet towel around.

464 When meeting someone for the first time, ask them what they like to do rather than what they do. It'll get them excited and make for better conversation.

465 Suspect someone is giving you the wrong phone number? Read it back to them incorrectly, and if they correct you, it's legit.

466 When filming video at a concert using your phone, put a finger over your phone's microphone. It'll sound clearer when you play it back.

467 Always buy the first pitcher or round of drinks. You'd be surprised how long you can drink on the phrase "I bought the first one."

468 Those lines on red Solo cups are actually alcohol measurements.

12 ounces
Beer

5 ounces
Wine

1 ounce
Liquor

469 If you're the designated driver, tell the bartender. Oftentimes, they'll give you soda and/or food for free!

470 When out with friends, place your phones stacked face-down in the middle of the table. First one to check their phone pays the bill!

471 Make flower-shaped ice by filling the bottom of any two-liter soda bottle with water and the food coloring of your choice. Freeze the bottle for a few hours and then cut it open to reveal the shaped ice.

472 A wineglass in a bowl makes for a great chips 'n' dip set.

CHAPTER 9

AROUND THE HOUSE

473 The best way to clean a microwave: Put a cup of hot water and vinegar inside, turn it on for three to five minutes, and wipe clean with ease.

474 Use a blow dryer to instantly defog any mirror.

475 Get a small pan and fill it with water. Add some vanilla extract and cinnamon and put it on the stove. Your house will smell like a delicious bakery in no time.

476 No dryer sheets? Throw in two tinfoil balls for static-free clothes every time.

477 Can't catch a fly? Spray it with Windex. This will immobilize it and make for an easy kill.

478 In a rush to dry your clothes? Throw a dry bath towel into the dryer along with your wet clothes. They'll dry much faster.

479 Sick of having a box of tangled cords? Use old toilet paper rolls to organize them.

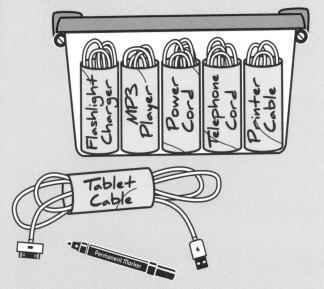

Flashlight Charger
MP3 Player
Power Cord
Telephone Cord
Printer Cable

Tablet Cable

Permanent Marker

7 UNUSUAL USES FOR TENNIS BALLS

480 Boots or heels leave a scuff mark on your floor? Rub a tennis ball over the mark and it'll come right out.

481 Run out of dryer sheets? Toss a few tennis balls in for a suitable replacement.

482 Keep your rainy day cash safe. Cut open a slit in a tennis ball, stuff in some money, and store it in a safe place. No burglar will ever steal a tennis ball!

483 Get rid of nasty goop and human oils from your pool by throwing in a tennis ball.

484 Back acting up? Lie on a tennis ball for a great DIY back massage.

485 Childproof those sharp table corners with a tennis ball that's been cut open halfway.

486 Hang a tennis ball from a piece of string in your garage so you know where to stop when parking your car.

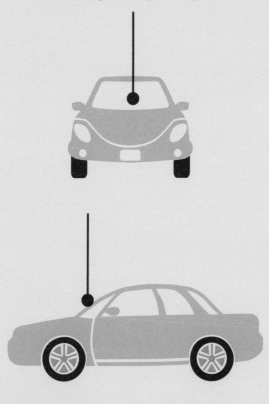

487 Take a picture of your fridge and pantry on your phone before you go grocery shopping. You'll never forget anything at the store again!

488 Put a magnet at the bottom of your hammer so you can stick nails to it. This is a great trick for when you're on a ladder or in an awkward space.

489 Looking for something? Scan right to left with your eyes. You'll pick up more since your brain isn't used to reading that way.

490 Putting a small amount of 7UP in a flower vase will surprisingly preserve them for much longer.

491 Put dryer sheets on the back of a fan while it's blowing. They'll stick to the back of it and make a room smell amazing.

492 When drilling, fold a Post-it note to catch the dust as it falls.

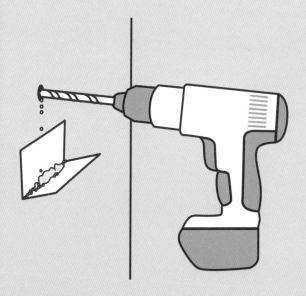

493 By adding a pinch of salt to your load of laundry you can actually brighten the colors of your clothes.

494 Put a used, wet sponge in the microwave for two minutes to kill 99% of the bacteria in it.

495 Need to sharpen your knives? Cut through some pieces of aluminum foil.

496 Got the sniffles? Take an empty tissue box and attach it to a full tissue box with elastic bands. Put your used tissues in the empty box and throw it away when it's full.

497 Broke a piece of glass? Put bread on it. The consistency of the bread will pick up even the smallest of shards.

498 If you want a streak-free shine on windows, use newspaper.

499 Dip the top of your keys in different-colored paint so you can easily tell them apart.

500 Clothes shrink too small? Soak them in a mixture of hot water and hair conditioner for five minutes and then air-dry them.

501 Hate that dust in the last couple bowls of cereal? Pour it into a strainer first. Problem solved!

502 Put old newspaper at the bottom of your trash bin. It will absorb any food juices and make for a cleaner disposal.

503 Did you know pots come with a built-in spoon holder? The slot at the end of the handle is perfect for holding on to spoons when you're not stirring the pot.

504 Sick of bathroom mirrors fogging up? Rub a little bit of soapy water on them before you hop into the shower.

505 Have flies in your house? They are attracted to bright lights. Use this knowledge to guide them out windows or your doors.

506 Need to iron a shirt but don't have the time? Hang it up in the bathroom as you shower. All the wrinkles will come out by the time you're done.

507 Drill a couple small holes in the lower side of a garbage can. This gets rid of any suction issues and will make putting in and taking out bags much easier.

508 Putting two hinges on one side of a painting is a perfect way to hide the thermostat while still having easy access to it.

509 Placing multiple ice cubes on your carpet can remove those annoying indentations left by tables, chairs, and other pieces of furniture.

510 The best way to remove pet hair from your carpet is to use a squeegee.

511 Place a rubber band over any stripped screw to easily unscrew it.

512 Out of Swiffer pads? Old socks work almost as well. Just make sure they're clean before you use them.

513 Clean up water stains easily by rubbing them with a sliced lemon.

514 Showerhead not working like it used to? Pour some white vinegar into a plastic bag and secure it to the head with a rubber band. Run the shower for a bit and it'll be good as new.

515 The best way to fold a T-shirt: Fold the bottom fourth of your shirt up. Place the left side of the shirt toward the center, folding at the shoulder, and do the same with the right side. Fold the right sleeve in toward the center so that the left side is folded neatly. Fold the bottom half of the shirt up and flip the entire shirt over, so that the folds are hidden beneath.

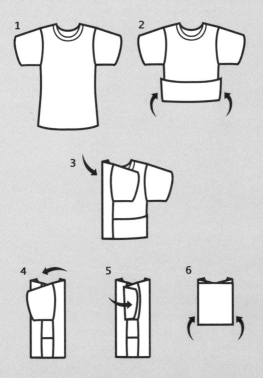

516 Food container smell bad even after you've washed it? Toss in a crunched-up piece of newspaper and leave it overnight. The smell will be gone by the morning.

517 Need a better grip on something like a jar, hammer, or screwdriver? Wrap a few rubber bands around it.

518 You can easily remove crayon marks from walls by dabbing a bit of gel-free toothpaste on them. Rub gently and then rinse it off with warm water.

519 Before hammering a nail into your wall, place a piece of sticky tape on the spot. This will prevent any chipping or cracking.

520 Believe it or not, rubbing a walnut on damaged wooden furniture can cover up a lot of dings and scratches.

CHAPTER 10

SCHOOL

521 Chew gum when you're studying, and then chew the same flavor when you take the test. This has been known to improve memory.

522 You're 50% more likely to remember something if you speak it out loud instead of simply reading it over and over.

523 Stumped on a project or presentation? Try ditching the computer and write by hand. The experience has been proven to help creativity.

524 Dorm room a little stinky? Put dry tea bags around your room. They will absorb the unpleasant odor.

525 Mathway.com solves all kinds of math homework problems with step-by-step explanations.

526 When doing a presentation in PowerPoint, always save it as a "PowerPoint Show" (.ppsx). This will open it directly to the slideshow.

527 Writing an essay? Copy and paste it into Google translate and have the computer read it out to you. It'll be much easier to find errors this way.

528 If your calculator runs out of batteries in the middle of an exam, rub the ends of the batteries together. This can give you up to an extra fifteen minutes of battery life.

529 Study your notes within one day of taking them. Retention rates are 60% higher then.

530 Paper due? Low on black ink? Change the font color to dark tan. It looks almost identical to black ink.

531 Keep pen thieves away: Put a blue ink cartridge in a red pen. No one steals red pens.

532 Taking a quick nap after learning something new can solidify that memory in your brain.

533 At Chegg.com, you can rent expensive textbooks online for a semester instead of buying them at a bookstore.

534 The EasyBib iPhone app will give you a bibliography on any book if you simply scan the barcode.

535 Stop using Google.com to search information for school essays. Use "scholar.google.com" instead. You'll find more relevant information right away.

536 Stumped on a question or math problem? Lie down. Your thought process is much faster when you're lying down, which is why you always lie down at psychiatrist appointments.

537 Want to find a good job after college? Make friends with as many people in your field that are on track to graduate one or two years ahead of you.

538 One of the best ways to study is to pretend that you're going to have to teach the material.

539 Send your resume as a .PDF file since it's much cleaner and more professional looking, unless specifically asked for a Word document.

540 Have a separate user account on your laptop for presentations. This way, embarrassing personal things won't show up when you open it up in class.

541 SelfControl is a program that blocks sites like Facebook, Twitter, and e-mail for a specified period of time. Using it will help you minimize distractions while you study or do homework.

542 When proofreading, read the document out loud to yourself. Your mouth will catch errors your mind might glance over.

543 Being surrounded by the color yellow will help you stay focused. Yellow decreases the production of melatonin, the hormone that makes you sleepy.

544 You are more likely to remember something you've written in blue ink than something you've written in black ink.

545 When doing long assignments, set a thirty-minute timer and race it. This will prevent you from procrastination.

546 Want to remember your notes more easily? Use a weird font style. Studies have shown the uniqueness of a font will make you more likely to remember what's written.

547 Need some good music to do homework to? Try video game or movie soundtracks. They're designed specifically to provide backgrounds that won't mess with your concentration.

548 It's actually better to take exams on an empty stomach. Hunger makes you focus better.

549 Eating chocolate while studying helps the brain retain new information more easily, and has been directly linked to higher test scores.

550 Learning a new language? Try to find a translation of your favorite book from when you were a kid.

551 If you're pulling an all-nighter, have a fifteen- to twenty-minute nap just before the sun comes up, and your body will reset itself.

552 When you graduate college or university, make sure to hold on to your college ID. You'll usually still be able to get student discounts because most places only look at the photo, not the graduation year.

553 Don't skimp on sleep. Sleep is more important than homework: It's proven that it's better to get a good sleep than to stay up late cramming for exams.

DID YOU ENJOY THIS BOOK?
WE'D LOVE TO HEAR FROM YOU!

Please send your comments to:
Hallmark Book Feedback
P.O. Box 419034
Mail Box 100
Kansas City, MO 64141

Or e-mail us at:
booknotes@hallmark.com